MOON

by Melanie Mitchell

↳ Lerner Publications Company · Minneapolis

Look up in the night sky.

What is that bright **glow?**

It is the **moon.**

The moon is Earth's **neighbor.**

Earth has only one moon.

Other planets have many
moons.

The moon is made of **rock.**

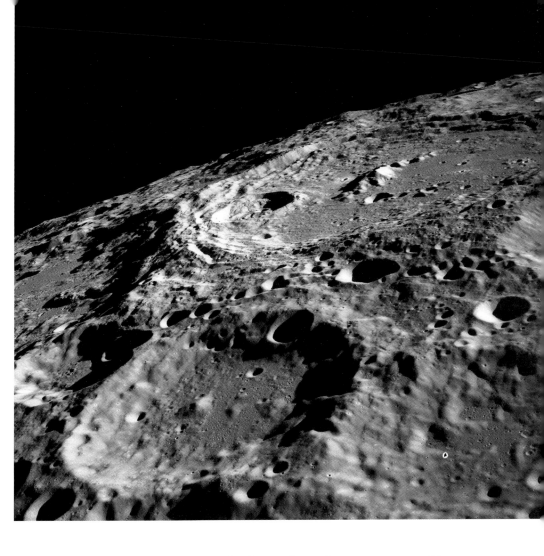

There are big holes on the
moon called **craters.**

The moon moves around
Earth.

It takes almost a month for the moon to circle Earth.

The sun makes the moon
glow so we can see it.

Sometimes we see the whole moon.

Sometimes we see half of the moon.

Sometimes we see only a little of the moon.

In 1969, people walked on the moon.

Maybe you can go to the
moon one day.

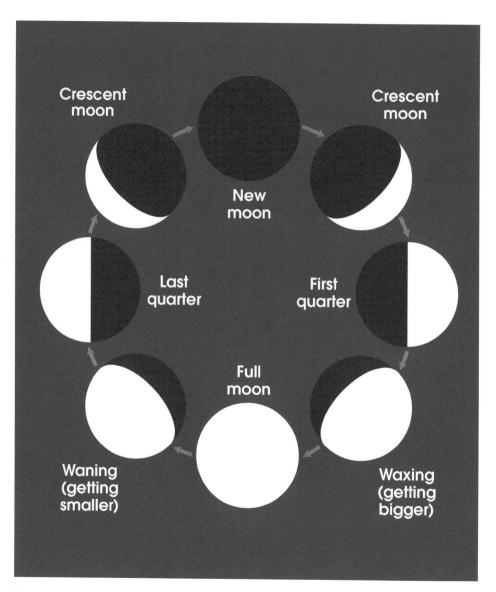

Phases of the Moon

The shape of the moon in the sky depends on how much sunlight shines on the moon. These different shapes are called the phases of the moon. When we see just a small part of the moon, it is called a crescent moon. When we see about half of the moon, it is called a quarter moon, and when we see the whole moon, it is called a full moon. It takes the moon between 28 and 30 days to go from a crescent moon to a full moon and back again.

Moon Fun Facts

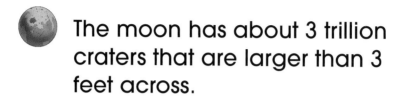 The moon has about 3 trillion craters that are larger than 3 feet across.

 The biggest crater on the moon is 140 miles wide.

The first person to walk on the moon was U.S. astronaut Neil Armstrong in 1969.

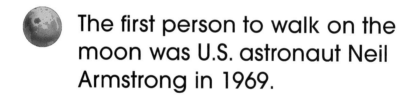 The moon turns at nearly the same speed as Earth. Because of this, the same side of the moon always faces Earth.

There is no air to breathe on the moon.

 The moon is the only place other than Earth in our solar system that humans have visited.

 It would take about 142 days to drive in a car going 70 miles per hour from Earth to the moon.

 When people can see the entire moon from Earth, it is called a full moon.

Glossary

 craters – holes in the ground that are shaped like bowls

 glow – to shine brightly

 moon – the heavenly body that revolves around Earth

 neighbor – someone or something that is next to or near another

 rock – a hard naturally formed material

Index

The photographs in this book are reproduced through the courtesy of: © Rob Matheson/CORBIS, front cover; © David Wrobel/Visuals Unlimited, p. 2; © Mark Newman/Visuals Unlimited, pp. 3, 22 (second from top); © Arthur Morris/Visuals Unlimited, pp. 4, 22 (middle); © Stock Image/SuperStock, pp. 5, 22 (second from bottom); © Barry Blackman/SuperStock, p. 6; © PhotoDisc Royalty-Free by Getty Images, pp. 7, 15, 17; © NASA, pp. 8, 9, 16, 22 (top, bottom); © Gunner Kullenberg/SuperStock, p. 10; © Robert Maust /Photo Agora, p. 11; © Gil Lopez-Espina/Visuals Unlimited, p. 12; © Bert Krages/Visuals Unlimited, p. 13; © W. A. Banaszewski/Visuals Unlimited, p. 14.

This book is available in two editions:
Library binding by Lerner Publications Company, a division of Lerner Publishing Group, Inc.
Soft cover by First Avenue Editions, an imprint of Lerner Publishing Group, Inc.
241 First Avenue North
Minneapolis, MN 55401 U.S.A.

Website address: www.lernerbooks.com

Library of Congress Cataloging-in-Publication Data

Mitchell, Melanie S.
    Moon / by Melanie Mitchell.
        p.   cm. — (First step nonfiction)
    Includes index.
    Summary: A simple introduction to earth's single moon.
    ISBN-13: 978–0–8225–0188–6 (lib. bdg. : alk. paper)
    ISBN-10: 0–8225–0188–0 (lib. bdg. : alk. paper)
    ISBN-13: 978–0–8225–3591–1 (pbk. : alk. paper)
    ISBN-10: 0–8225–3591–2 (pbk. : alk. paper)
    1. Moon—Juvenile literature. [1. Moon.] I. Title. II. Series.
QB582.M58 2004
523.3—dc21   2003005631

Manufactured in the United States of America
5 – DP – 10/1/09